Benjamin Franklin: 1706-1790
"A Chronology of the Eighteenth Century's Most Eminent Citizen!"

Compiled by Frank B. Jones
Past President
The Friends of Franklin, Inc.

With Assistance from Tully Shaw and George F. Waters

Benjamin Franklin: 1706-1790
"A Chronology of the Eighteenth Century's Most Eminent Citizen!"

Compiled by Frank B. Jones
Past President
The Friends of Franklin, Inc.

With Assistance from Tully Shaw and
George F. Waters

Edited for Publication by The Friends of Franklin, Inc., Dr. Larry E. Tise, Executive Director, Benjamin Franklin National Memorial of The Franklin Institute. Assistant Editor, Layout, and Design by Francine Britton. Photography, except as noted, by Charles Penniman.

KENDALL/HUNT PUBLISHING COMPANY
4050 Westmark Drive   Dubuque, Iowa 52002

With thanks to Virginia D. Ward, Library Assistant, The Franklin Institute and John V. Alviti, Senior Curator, The Franklin Institute.

Cover photograph "Gray Coat" - Portrait by Joseph Siffred Duplessis, NPG. 87:43. Gift of the Morris and Gwendolyn Cafritz Foundation. Courtesy of The National Portrait Gallery, Washington, D.C.

Copyright © 1996 by The Friends of Franklin, Inc.

ISBN 0-7872-2517-7

All rights reserved. No part of this publication may be reproduced, stored in a retrieval system, or transmitted, in any form or by any means, electronic, mechanical, photocopying, recording, or otherwise, without the prior written permission of the copyright owner.

Printed in the United States of America
10 9 8 7 6 5 4 3 2 1

This book is dedicated in memoriam
to William George Carr, 1901-1966.
Died March 1, 1996.
The most faithful Friend of Franklin.

PREFACE by Frank B. Jones

I expect you would agree that a majority of Americans nowadays know very little about what went on in this world before they were born. Actually, to most people, young and old, learning about the beginnings of our nation might be considered a bore! Yet we all seem to agree that *TRUTH CAN BE MORE INTERESTING THAN FICTION!* This is definitely the case when we contemplate the lifetime of America's most famous man of the eighteenth century. What follows here is a newly designed effort to evoke a new curiosity in you, the reader, regarding Dr. Benjamin Franklin of Philadelphia and the world.

This most interesting of history's characters happens to be the only founding father of our country who signed all four of the most important documents leading up to our independence (i.e., The Albany Plan, The Declaration of Independence, The Treaty of Peace with England, and the United States Constitution). And he was involved up to his bifocal glasses in all four of these important events!

Many of us know that Benjamin Franklin was a printer from Philadelphia who our elderly friends remember as the founder of the <u>Saturday Evening Post</u> (which hasn't been proven). That about completes most people's knowledge, except for some who know that Dr. Franklin was a big hit with the ladies of France and that he wrote a long list of humorous and valid truisms for inclusion in his widely read <u>Poor Richard's Almanac</u>. Yet there is much more to his long life. For example, when he met all of those French ladies, he was a widower in his seventies!

It is unfortunate that Americans know so little about the beginnings of our nation. Our country is a young nation compared to many nations of the globe. But yet, in truth, ours is the oldest land in the world in which citizens have held the power to govern. Let us give credit to our nation's founders. They left us a nation with more freedoms for each of us to enjoy than existed in other countries. But even Franklin himself challenged all of us that we would have to work at it in order to keep these fragile freedoms functioning!

Some of us who have long studied Benjamin Franklin like to point out that to know about Franklin and his life is to know the story of how our nation was founded. He was, without a doubt, the most central figure in that grand drama. That is not to take anything away from George Washington, Thomas Jefferson, John Adams, James Madison, John Jay, Alexander Hamilton or anyone else. It is just that Franklin was at center stage for a longer period of time than were any of those other characters. Just living eighty-four years was no mean feat. But to be of service to others for all of those years is nothing short of remarkable!

He was the best-known American in the world during his lifetime. To know of his personality, his character, his disappointments, challenges, wit and wisdom, and above all his accomplishments, is a challenge which we hope we can help you undertake. This brief chronicle of Dr. Franklin's life comes in easy to read outline form which can be covered in a short time. But don't hurry! Absorb it as you read. And refer to it again and again. Although his life is presented chronologically, we emphasize accomplishments over dates and places. Our approach highlights a long and fruitful lifetime that we hope, once you have had this taste, you will want to know much, much more about this incredibly gifted man's experiences!

So it is with high aspiration and expectation that we challenge everyone from middle school to retirement years to make an investment in knowledge by spending a bit of time absorbing the fascinating and awesome eighteenth century life of Benjamin Franklin, printer. And humanitarian genius.   ...FBJ

THE CHRONOLOGY

1706: On January 17th (new style calendar) Benjamin Franklin is born in Boston, Massachusetts, the youngest son in the family. BF's father, Josiah Franklin (1658-1745) has emigrated from England primarily for religious reasons. Josiah has 17 children by two wives. BF's mother, Abiah Folger Franklin (1667-1752), Josiah's second wife, was born and raised on Nantucket Island.

1714: BF attends Boston Grammar School and Brownell's English School.

1716: BF assists his father, a candle maker and soap boiler. Josiah removes BF from school after only two years. At age 10 he is already an avid reader.

1718: BF apprenticed to his half-brother, James, to learn the printing trade. James is, at this time, printer for The Boston Gazette. Writes a ballad, "The Lighthouse Tragedy," and publishes it by himself as a broadside.

1719: BF borrows books by John Bunyan, Daniel Defoe, and John Locke from friends. Writes and publishes another ballad "On the Taking of Teach or Blackbeard the Pirate."

1721: James launches his own newspaper, The New-England Courant devoted to humor, literature, and opinion.

1722: Unaware of who might be the author, James prints in his newspaper fourteen anonymous "tongue in cheek" essays about life in Massachusetts by a "Mrs. Silence Dogood." These famous essays, written by BF at age 16, have often been reprinted as examples of BF's literary ability. BF manages the Courant for nearly a month while

James is imprisoned for his editorial attacks on local officials. BF tries unsuccessfully to become a vegetarian, partly to save money to buy books.

1723: BF becomes again temporary editor of the Courant when James refuses to be censored and goes into hiding to avoid arrest. Differences with his brother and harsh treatment by James cause BF to run away to New York where he is not able to find work. He then travels to Philadelphia by walking across New Jersey, arriving on October 6. BF finds work in Samuel Keimer's Philadelphia print shop. BF rents lodging from John Reed, father of his future wife, Deborah. Mrs. Reed cautions her daughter about the budding courtship.

1724: BF visits his parents in Boston and meets the revered clergyman Cotton Mather. In Philadelphia he meets Governor William Keith who promises him money and political help in beginning a printing business. BF borrows money and travels to London, England, to buy a printing press and other equipment. When Keith's letters of introduction and credit prove to be worthless, BF is forced to find work as a printer to pay his passage back to America.

1725: Deborah Reed, having heard nothing from BF, marries John Rogers in Philadelphia. Rogers disappears four months later, never to return or make contact. BF continues to work as a printer in London.

1726: BF returns to Philadelphia, keeping a journal during the voyage, July 22 to October 11. He takes employment in the mercantile store of fellow-passenger Thomas Denham. Keith is no longer the governor.

1727: Denham dies, while BF suffers severely with pleurisy. BF returns to the printing trade again with Samuel Keimer. He founds the Junto, a self-improvement and community service club in Philadelphia. Keimer sends BF to nearby Burlington, NJ, to manage his print shop there.

1728: BF prints paper money for the colony of New Jersey. BF then resigns to form a printing partnership with Hugh Meredith in Philadelphia. BF writes his own personal religious creed, "Articles of Belief and Acts of Religion."

1729: BF buys a failing newspaper, <u>The Pennsylvania Gazette</u>, and begins to make it the largest circulating paper in the American colonies.

1730: BF's first child, William, is born out of wedlock (the precise date is unknown). Franklin forms a common-law union with Deborah Reed Rogers since the whereabouts of John Rogers are unknown and she cannot legally remarry. William is taken into the household. BF begins his studies of the French and German languages. BF is named official printer for the colony of Pennsylvania. BF borrows money to buy out his partner Meredith.

1731: BF leads in the establishment of the Library Company of Philadelphia, the first circulating library in North America (still in existence). He becomes a lifelong Mason, joining St. John's Lodge in Philadelphia. BF establishes in Charleston, S. C., the first of many remote printing partnerships.

1732: He publishes the first annual edition of <u>Poor Richard's Almanack</u> and prints the first German language newspaper in America. BF's second son, Francis Folger Franklin, is born. BF publishes an article complaining about the long sermons preached by Presbyterian ministers.

Press operated by Benjamin Franklin when he was apprenticed to his brother, James Franklin. Courtesy of the Massachusetts Charitable Mechanics Society.

Lady Chapel, Priory Church of Saint Bartholomew the Great in London. Franklin worked in a print shop located here. Postcard courtesy of Larry E. Tise.

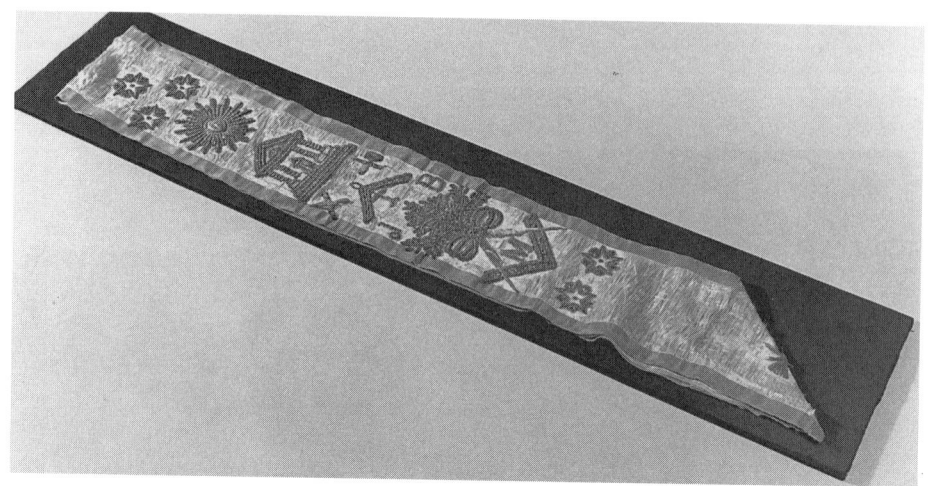

Masonic Sash said to belong to BF and worn during the years he was most active in French Free Masonry in the Lodge of the Nine Muses. Courtesy of the Masonic Library and Museum of Pennsylvania.

1733: BF designs a rigorous self-regimen and style of life to "arrive at moral perfection." He studies Italian, Spanish, and Latin.

1734: BF is elected grand master of Masons in Pennsylvania.

1735: After several fires, BF in the Pennsylvania Gazette calls for the establishment of volunteer fire-fighting societies in Philadelphia. He publicly supports the Reverend Samuel Hemphill, a popular Presbyterian minister who fellow clergy think emphasizes "good Christian" morals too much in his religious teachings. After Hemphill is denounced and suspended by the Presbyterian hierarchy, BF leaves the congregation, although he continues to support it financially. BF suffers another attack of pleurisy. He proposes the organization of a night watch in Philadelphia.

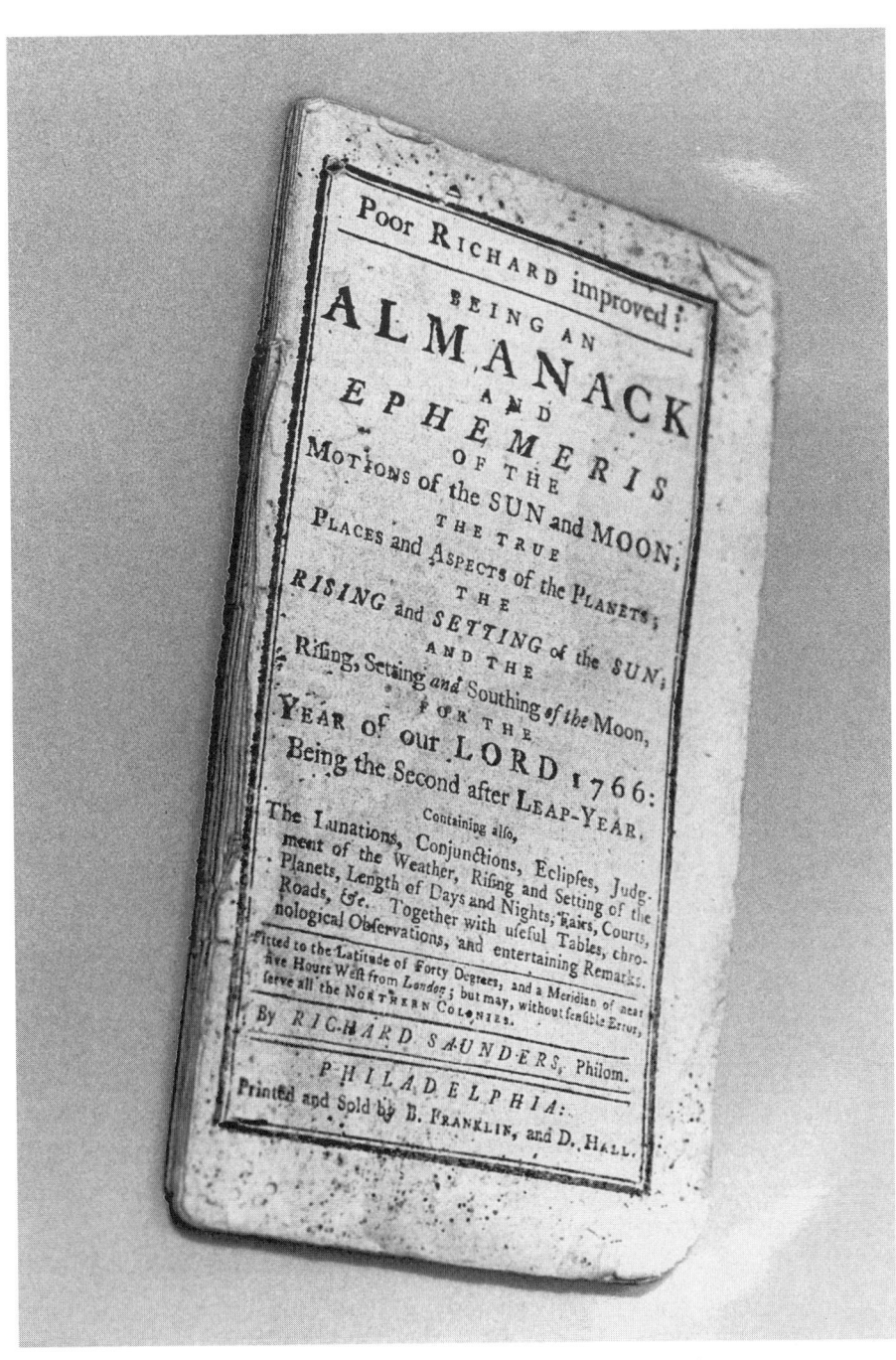

Poor Richard's Almanack, 1766. Courtesy of The Franklin Institute.

1736: BF's second son, Francis Folger Franklin, age four, dies of smallpox. BF is chosen clerk of the Pennsylvania Assembly. He devises a method to prevent counterfeiting of paper money. He prints money for New Jersey in his printing establishment in Burlington, NJ. Organizes the Union Fire Company, Philadelphia's first.

1737: BF is appointed postmaster of Philadelphia beginning October 7 and serves in this capacity for 16 years while still functioning as the clerk of the Pennsylvania Assembly and head of his printing and publishing business.

1739: The famous evangelist, George Whitefield, comes to Philadelphia and attracts large crowds. Franklin befriends him, measures the distance traveled by his voice, and begins publishing his sermons.

1740: BF becomes the official printer for New Jersey. Accuses another Philadelphia printer, Andrew Bradford, of pilfering his idea of publishing the first magazine in America. BF then undercut his competitor with a lower price.

1741: BF studies stoves and chimneys and designs what he calls the Pennsylvania fireplace. He does not patent the invention, wishing it to be adopted generally. BF publishes <u>The General Magazine and Historical Chronicle</u>, the second magazine to be published in America.

1742: BF opens a new printing partnership in New York City. He helps organize a project to fund the botanical expeditions of Philadelphia naturalist, John Bartram. Later, from Europe, he sends Bartram seeds of various vegetables to be introduced in America, including rhubarb and kohlrabi.

1743: BF calls for development of "useful knowledge" in a paper he publishes, resulting in the establishment of the

Colonial Paper Currency printed by BF and D. Hall with warning note "To Counterfeit is Death." Courtesy of The Franklin Institute.

American Philosophical Society. Several Junto members are elected charter members of this first organized American scientific society. Traveling to New England he begins a lifelong friendship with Cadwallader Colden, a New York botanist. He also enters into business with William Strahan, a British printer and businessman. Franklin's third and last child, his only daughter, Sarah, (Sally), is born August 31.

1744: David Hall, a young English printer, on BF's encouragement emigrates from England and becomes a printer with BF. BF publishes a reprint of the novel Pamela, by Samuel Richardson, the first novel printed in America.

1745: BF begins to experiment with electricity, opening correspondence with Englishman Peter Collinson who keeps BF informed about the status of electrical experiments being conducted in Europe. BF's father, Josiah, dies in Boston at age 87. BF publishes a woodcut depiction of the

The title page of the *Charters of Pennsylvania and Philadelphia*, 1742. Much of Franklin's wealth was derived from the printing of state documents for Pennsylvania and other colonies. Courtesy of The Franklin Institute.

The Pennsylvania Fire Place, popularly kown as "The Franklin Stove." A wooden replica with the right side panel removed to show the internal baffeling. The box that forms the stove's back heated air which was communicated to the room through parts in the stove's side panels. Courtesy of The Franklin Institute.

city of Louisbourg, the first newspaper illustration published in America.

1746: BF is reported to be "immersed in Electrical Experiments."

1747: Franklin develops his theory of the nature of electricity--which becomes known as the "Franklinian Theory"--and reports the results of his research to Collinson who, in turn, presents it to the British Royal Society. BF publishes a pamphlet entitled Plain Truth, disclosing Pennsylvania's vulnerability to the expansion of French and Indian military activity on the western frontier and on the

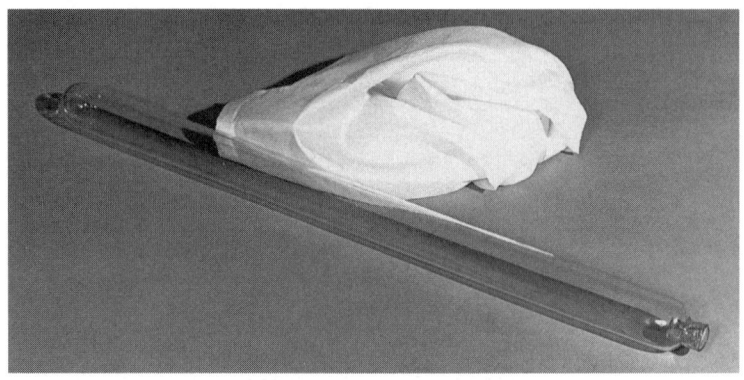

The long glass tube which, when rubbed with a silk cloth, separated electrical charges. Used by BF in his early electrical experiments prior to his building of the more convenient electrostatic machine. Courtesy of The Franklin Institute.

eastern seacoast. He leads in the organization of a Pennsylvania volunteer militia to defend settlers on the frontier in the face of several massacres and despite opposition from the large Quaker community.

1748: BF refuses the rank of colonel in the Pennsylvania militia to serve instead as a common soldier. BF grants equal partnership in his printing business to David Hall in exchange for Hall operating the business and for 50% of future profits. Establishing a longtime and very successful business partnership, BF retires from active business operations a wealthy man at age 42. He devotes the second half of his long life to scientific study, research, civic affairs, and international diplomacy. He moves his residence away from his shop and acquires the first of several black slaves he will own over the next thirty years. He is elected an alderman on the Philadelphia City Council.

1749: BF's electrical experiments with lightning rods enables him to demonstrate the value of lightning rods as protection against storm damage. He is the first person to refer to "negative and positive charges" of electricity. Although he designs and installs the first lightning rod, he never seeks a

Franklin's Electrostatic Machine, 1745. Courtesy of The Franklin Institute.

patent on the device. BF becomes Grand Master of the Mid-Atlantic province of Masonry. He writes and publishes a booklet entitled <u>Proposals Relating to the Education of Youth in Pensilvania</u>. These proposals result in the founding of an academy which becomes the University of Pennsylvania, established formally in 1751. BF serves for many years as a trustee.

1750: BF suffers his first of several attacks of the gout. He revises his plans for lightning rods by attaching a ground wire. Continues his electrical experiments, including one in which he is severely shocked while demonstrating how to electrocute a turkey. Lightning rods come into fashion in America and Europe.

1751: BF is elected to the Pennsylvania Assembly which then appoints him as commissioner to draw up a treaty with the Pennsylvania Indians at Carlisle. BF's <u>Experiments and Observations on Electricity</u> is published in first edition in London. In Philadelphia, BF and Dr. Thomas Bond establish the first public hospital in the colonies, the innovative Pennsylvania Hospital. It is initially funded with BF's unique legislative proposal for a grant of public funds to be matched with private funds. The hospital continues into the present. Franklin's experiments in electricity are widely published in Europe. BF initiates discussions among several fire companies to form the first fire insurance company in America called the Pennsylvania Contributionship.

1752: BF's mother, Abiah Folger, dies in Boston at age 84. BF in June devises and carries out a kite experiment to collect electrical charges during thunderstorm conditions thereby proving the identicalness of lightning and electricity. The <u>Pennsylvania Gazette</u> carries an explanation on how to build and install BF's lightning rod. To assist his brother John who is suffering with bladder stones, BF devises, out of silver, the first flexible catheter.

1753: Franklin is appointed Joint Deputy Postmaster General of North America. Inspects the postal routes in New England and, while there, receives honorary degrees from Yale and Harvard. Negotiates a treaty at Carlisle, Pa., with several Indian tribes and then publishes the contents of the treaties. For his work on electricity, BF is awarded the Copley medal by Britain's Royal Society, its most prestigious medal.

1754: French and Indian massacres on Pennsylvania's western frontier flare up again. BF draws and publishes America's first newspaper cartoon showing a snake cut into sections over the caption, "Join or Die," signifying that the colonies should join together to protect the lives of settlers on the western frontier. Britain at the time had shown little interest in a military response to French and Indian acts of violence. BF represents Pennsylvania at a conference attended by representatives of seven colonies at Albany,

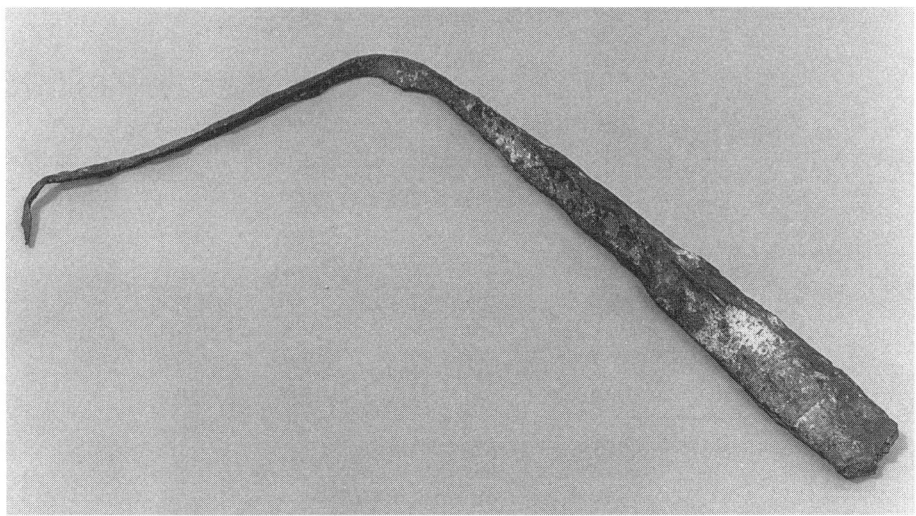

Wrought Iron Lightning Rod salvaged from John Wister's house, one of the first buildings to be protected from lightning by Franklin after BF determined that lightning and the "electrical fluid" produced in his electrical experiments were the same and so could be discharged through the use of points. Courtesy of The Franklin Institute.

Title page from *Experiments and Observations in Electricity*. Courtesy of The Franklin Institute.

New York. He proposes a joint military partnership known as the Albany Plan to counteract French and Indian raids, the first proposal that British colonies unite. Although adopted at the conference, the plan is rejected by the assemblies of the seven colonies and by the British government. BF's electrical experiments continue to be published at home and abroad. He sends a letter to the Royal Governor of Massachusetts protesting the taxing of people who have no representation in the legislative body voting on tax levies.

1755: BF meets with General Braddock, commander of the British forces in America sent to protect lives on the frontier. BF pledges a large sum of his personal wealth to obtain needed equipment for Braddock's campaign in western Pennsylvania in the French and Indian War. The Pennsylvania Assembly passes BF's bill establishing a militia. After Braddock's defeat he is appointed Commissioner by the Assembly to oversee the construction of forts on the western frontier and he is elected Colonel by the regiment of foot recruited in Philadelphia during the emergency. He

Odometer used by Franklin. When attached to a carriage, it would show the distances traveled. Used by Franklin to measure postal routes. Courtesy of The Franklin Institute.

17

travels extensively in western Pennsylvania and New York in these capacities.

1756: BF is appointed as a military commissioner for Northampton County, Pennsylvania. He introduces a successful program of street paving, lighting, and cleaning in Philadelphia. The College of William and Mary confers an honorary degree on him. BF conducts military inspections at Carlisle, Pennsylvania and in New York. He and other commissioners meet with Indians of the Delaware tribe in Easton, Pennsylvania. BF joins with Quakers in attempting to compel the Penn family to pay taxes on their Pennsylvania properties. He is elected a Fellow of the British Royal Society and a member of the Society for the Encouragement of Arts, Manufactures and Commerce in London.

The Copley Medal as pictured in the December 1753 issue of *The Gentlemen's Magazine*. Awarded by the Royal Society to Benjamin Franklin, November 30, 1753 and "...delivered to be transmitted to him by the care of his worthy friend P. Collinson, Esq.; fellow of the said Society." Courtesy of The Free Library of Philadelphia.

1757: The Pennsylvania Assembly decides to support the project to make the Penn lands taxable. BF is appointed agent of the colony in London to press King George III and

18

Parliament to approve the Assembly's request. Deborah, BF's wife, chooses not to accompany BF on his trip to Britain. But BF takes his son, William, who will attend law school in London. He writes his famous work, "The Way to Wealth," during his voyage. BF meets with Pennsylvania proprietors, Thomas and Richard Penn. BF finds the lodging he would use during sixteen years in London at 32 Craven Street with a widow, Margaret Stevenson, and her daughter, Mary (called Polly).

1758: BF writes his 25th and final annual edition of <u>Poor Richard's Almanack</u>, sending it for publication to his partner, David Hall, in Philadelphia. BF meets with British officials about the Penn family tax problem. In recognition of his fame as a scientist, BF is invited to meet and socialize with many prominent English citizens, such as James Cook, Richard Price, William Strahan, Joseph Priestley, James Boswell, David Hume, and others. He is also invited to join many scientific and literary organizations. BF and son travel to Northamptonshire to locate relatives living in and around Ecton, birthplace of BF's father, Josiah. They locate relatives and find family graves in Ecton churchyard. In November, the Penn family agrees to pay taxes as outlined in a compromise proposed by BF. Continues experiments on heat conduction. BF invents a chimney damper.

1759: BF receives an honorary doctorate at University of St. Andrews in Scotland. He visits Edinburgh and receives an official welcome as a "Burgess and Gild Brother." Even though his formal education is only at the primary level, BF is thereafter commonly referred to as "Doctor Franklin." His friend, Richard Jackson, whom he met through Peter Collinson, urges BF to run for a seat in the British Parliament. Later, Jackson will support the American colonies in Parliament. BF takes a lengthy tour of northern England and Scotland meeting Lord Kames, William Robertson, and Adam Smith.

1760: A third expanded edition of Franklin's electrical observations is published in London. BF writes a pamphlet on the importance of Canada to Britain and to the colonies. At the meeting of a group he joins, called the Associates of Dr. Bray, which raises money for the education of blacks in America, he meets Samuel Johnson among other notables.

1761: BF becomes an active and influential member in the Royal Society's committee to study agricultural methods through the exchange of plants between England and the American colonies. He travels with son William and Richard Jackson to Belgium and Holland. In London he attends the coronation of King George III.

Craven Street House, Circa 1995.
Photograph by Larry E. Tise

1762: BF receives an honorary doctorate from Oxford University. He invents a new musical instrument which he calls the "glass armonica." Mozart and Beethoven later compose works for the instrument. BF departs in the fall for Philadelphia. His son, William, remains in London to marry English-born Elizabeth Downes. Five days after the marriage, September 9, William, then a lawyer, is named Royal Governor of New Jersey. In Philadelphia, the Pennsylvania Assembly honors BF for his services in London.

1763: As Deputy Postmaster General he travels extensively in northern colonies conducting post office inspections and establishing postal routes. BF visits the British-sponsored school for blacks in Philadelphia and writes, "I have conceived a higher opinion of the natural capacities of the black race than I have ever before entertained."

Benjamin Franklin's Glass Armonica. Courtesy of The Franklin Institute.
Photograph by J. J. Barton.

1764: BF is elected Speaker of the Pennsylvania Assembly. He drafts a pamphlet denouncing the "Paxton Boys" who committed a massacre of friendly Indians in Lancaster County, Pennsylvania. He writes a letter to all British colonial assemblies asking them to oppose the Stamp Act tax, and signs the letter as Speaker of the Pennsylvania Assembly. BF is defeated for reelection to the Pennsylvania Assembly after a bitterly fought election. The Assembly, nevertheless, reappoints him to be their agent in London to oppose the Stamp Tax. Deborah Franklin again chooses not to accompany him. BF arrives in London on December 9 and moves back into Margaret Stevenson's house on Craven Street.

1765: The Stamp Act becomes law, yet is later delayed by court action; but not before violent protest gets underway in the colonies. An angry mob believing Franklin actually supports the act is barely averted from attacking his Philadelphia home with Deborah inside. He does succeed in having Parliament eliminate the British army's practice of quartering British troops in private homes in America. He writes dozens of protest articles against the Act.

1766: BF's partnership agreement with his printing partner, David Hall, expires. Hall, very successful, buys out Franklin's share of the business. BF is examined before the entire House of Commons sitting as a Committee of the Whole. His testimony on American views of the Stamp Act proves crucial in the repeal of the act nine days later on February 22. BF accompanies Dr. John Pringle, later to become physician to the Queen of England, on a visit to Holland and Germany. In Gottingen, BF is elected to the German Academy of Sciences.

1767: BF is appointed member of a royal commission in London to settle a boundary dispute between New York and New Jersey. BF visits Paris with Dr. Pringle. They are formally presented to the French King, Louis XV, in the Palace at Versailles. BF's daughter, Sally, marries English-born Richard Bache in Philadelphia against her father's wishes.

1768: Georgia Assembly appoints BF as it's agent to the British government. BF writes a history of the problems between Britain and the colonies titled <u>Causes of the American Discontents</u>. He also devises a phonetic alphabet for the English language and tests it in letters to Mary Stevenson. He also compiles data he has collected on his five crossings of the Atlantic Ocean and publishes the first map outlining the direction, course, and size of the Gulf Stream.

1769: The fourth and further enlarged edition of BF's <u>Experiments and Observations on Electricity</u> is published in London. He is elected (in absentia) president of the American Philosophical Society in Philadelphia and is reelected each year for the rest of his life. BF's wife, Deborah, has a stroke which handicaps her severely for the rest of her life. BF joins with others in forming the Ohio Company to obtain Ohio land grants to be sold speculatively to potential settlers. The New Jersey House of Representatives appoints BF as its agent in Britain. His grandson, Benjamin Franklin Bache, is born to Sally in Philadelphia. BF writes an important paper on defining the position of American colonies on taxation without representation to be circulated privately among selected members of Parliament.

1770: The General Assembly of Massachusetts appoints BF as its agent as well, giving him a total of four colonies, Pennsylvania, Georgia, New Jersey, and Massachusetts.

1771: Lord Hillsborough, British secretary for colonial affairs, refuses to recognize BF as a colonial agent despite the fact that he was elected by all four legislatures. Hillsborough rules that only the governors of each colony can appoint its official agent. Franklin ignores Hillsborough's ruling. BF visits his good friend Bishop Jonathan Shipley at his country estate, Twyford, where he would later begin writing the first section of his famous <u>Autobiography</u>. With his friend, Richard Jackson, he visits Ireland and Scotland. In Ireland he witnesses the opening of the Irish Parliament. In Edinburgh he stays with Lord Kames and David Hume. On his return to London BF meets son-in-law, Richard Bache and his family, for the first time. BF donates what he calls "many valuable books" to Harvard University.

1772: BF is elected one of only eight foreign members of the Royal Academy of Sciences of France. The Ohio Land Company deal sought by BF fails as lands were never officially conveyed to be sold. Following the judgement in the Sommersett Case in Britain--which frees all slaves on the British Islands--BF writes that slavery is evil and unjust and that the judgement should be extended to the British colonies in America. BF, given copies of letters written by Massachusetts Royal Governor Thomas Hutchinson to British officials calling for the repression of unrest in that colony, covertly sends copies back to Thomas Cushing, Speaker of the Massachusetts Assembly, requesting confidentiality.

1773: The Massachusetts Assembly "leaks" information about the Hutchinson letters and the letters themselves. The British government seeks to find the person who "stole" the letters. A possible charge of treason is rumored to be imminent for BF. In counterattack BF files a petition with Lord Dartmouth calling for removal of Governor Hutchinson. BF, the consummate revolutionary, then writes and publishes a paper entitled "Rules By Which A Great Empire May Be Reduced to a Small One" to show the folly of British policy. Almost symbolically, BF proceeds then to conduct experiments on the use of oil to calm waters in the fall of a rough year.

Chart showing the Gulf stream (sic: "Gulph Stream") as printed in Franklin's "Maritime Observations," *Philosophical and Miscellaneous Papers.*
Courtesy of The Franklin Institute.

1774: News of the Boston Tea Party reaches London in January. Later BF offers to pay for the loss of the tea. At a Privy Council session, BF is called forward and is labeled a thief and denounced by Solicitor General Alexander Wedderburn. BF refuses to respond and he soon loses his position as Deputy Postmaster General for North America. BF publishes a paper called, "Hints For a Durable Union Between England and America." The colonies petition King George III about the unfairness of Parliament's approach to the tax problem and send petitions to BF to deliver to the King. Negotiations on the dispute prove futile. Deborah Franklin has another stroke and dies on December 19, aged 66. The First Continental Congress begins its meetings in Philadelphia on September 5.

1775: On February 9, Parliament declares Massachusetts to be in rebellion. Rumors of BF's impending arrest abound. BF embarks for Philadelphia, arriving May 5. During voyage BF conducts temperature experiments and and determines that the Gulf Stream temperature is consistently warmer than the surrounding ocean water. BF is immediately chosen a Pennsylvania delegate to the Second Continental Congress. He drafts the Articles of Confederation--the first Constitution of the United States--and submits them, but Congress delays their approval. BF designs paper money and submits resolutions proposing free trade among the colonies. These are adopted. In October, BF is sent to confer with General Washington in Cambridge, Massachusetts, about the needs of the army. He returns to Philadelphia November 9, accompanying his sister Jane Mecom to Rhode Island, as she flees the British occupation of Boston. BF is appointed a member of the powerful Committee of Secret Correspondence dealing with foreign policy. He is also appointed to a committee to write a "Declaration by the United Colonies of North America"--not the Declaration of Independence. He is unanimously elected Postmaster General of the Colonies. He serves on a total of ten Congressional committees.

1776: BF celebrates his 70th birthday on Jan. 17th. He writes an appeal to the French Government for aid and gives American representative Silas Deane instructions on how to deliver it. BF is appointed a Commissioner to Canada to negotiate an alliance. Still believing in the importance of Canada to the United States, BF leads an official party to Montreal to make Canada an ally against England. The mission fails. He serves as a member of the Pennsylvania Constitutional Convention. On June 11 he is appointed to the committee of Congress with Thomas Jefferson to write the Declaration of Independence. BF is present in Congress for the completion and approval of the Declaration. He

Terra-cotta Medallion by Nini, showing Franklin in his famous fur hat. This medallion is an example of the souvenir items attesting to Franklin's popularity in France. This popularity contributed to his success in persuading the French government to assist the American cause in the American Revolution. Courtesy of The Franklin Institute.

signs the Declaration in a bold and unmistakable hand. He is appointed with John Adams and Edward Rutledge to confer with his old acquaintance, British Admiral Lord Richard Howe, on Staten Island, New York. The meeting solves nothing. BF is unanimously elected as one of the three commissioners to the court of France. He loans almost 4000 pounds to Congress as an example of confidence to encourage others to do likewise. The New Jersey militia arrests and imprisons his son, Royal Governor William Franklin, a leading Loyalist. BF declines to intercede for his son. BF departs on his seventh and most dangerous Atlantic crossing on October 27, arriving on the west coast of France on December 3. Grandsons, William Temple Franklin, William's son, and Benjamin Franklin Bache, Sally's son, accompany him. Upon his arrival BF proceeds directly to Paris to meet with French Foreign Minister Comte de Vergennes.

Benjamin Franklin's bold signature. Courtesy of The Franklin Institute.

1777: BF turns down an appointment as Commissioner also to Spain, citing his age and health. Secretly France loans 2,000,000 livres to the American Congress. BF settles in Passy, then a Paris suburb, in the fashionable home of the wealthy Jacques-Donatien Leray de Chaumont. Grandson William Temple Franklin becomes secretary to Franklin and the Commission. Young Benjamin Franklin Bache attends school first in Passy and then in Geneva.

The war continues to go badly for Americans. The goals of the American commissioners are twofold: to obtain foreign money and to bring France and Spain into the war against England. BF becomes active in French society in and around Paris and also became very popular with the French people who quickly recognize him "by his Quaker appearance." His likeness begins to appear on large numbers of small chinaware keepsakes, terra cotta medallions, and medals bearing his profile and name. Thousands are produced and sold in France. BF speaks the French language with some difficulty, but writes it more satisfactorily. Colleagues Silas Deane, Arthur Lee, Ralph Izard and later John Adams do not share BF's popularity. French Foreign Minister Vergennes refuses to work with the often petulant Adams. To the French people BF's physical

Franklin in the Chamber of Parliament in London before the Lords in Council. Being questioned and mocked about the Boston Tea Party.
Courtesy of The American Philosophical Society.

The Franklin Flag with its seven pointed stars, one for each of the thirteen colonies and its thirteen stripes oddly arranged, but possibly with some numerological significance, now lost. Franklin designed the flag in France at about the time the Continental Congress adopted the "Betsy Ross" flag. Franklin made the flag to identify American war ships and to establish that they were not pirates. This flag was the first American flag to be recognized by a foreign power. Courtesy of The Franklin Institute.

appearance and demeanor symbolize individual freedom and stir among them a desire for the kind of liberty that seems to reign in America. American privateers begin capturing British ships and crews, often from French ports. Britain accuses France of harboring the privateers. BF and the other Commissioners approve the appointment of Jonathan Williams, Jr., BF's grand-nephew, as the American Agent for purchasing goods in Nantes, a strategic French Atlantic port. Many years later Williams will become the first commandant of West Point.

Washington's victories at Trenton and Princeton and in northern New Jersey eventually provide a better atmosphere for negotiating with the French government. BF is elected to the Royal Society of Medicine of France on June 17.

1778: The victory at Saratoga paves the way for the signing of a Treaty of Amity and Commerce and the alliance with France on February 6. On June 17 France goes to war with Britain. BF then becomes sole minister plenipotentiary to France on September 14. An office, a pension for life, and a peerage are offered to BF by a British secret agent in return for his betrayal of the American cause. BF treats the proposal with disdain. As Minister Plenipotentiary, he obtains additional critical loans from the government of France. He assists in the initiation of the famed philosopher Francois Marie Arouet Voltaire at the Masonic Lodge in Paris named "The Lodge of the Nine Sisters." BF and Voltaire embrace each other during a meeting of the French Academy of Sciences. When Voltaire dies, BF officiates at his Masonic commemoration on November 28. John Adams replaces Silas Deane as Commissioner and joins BF in Paris.

1779: BF announces another loan of 3,000,000 livres from the French government. Spain declares war on England on June 21. In London, BF's friend Benjamin Vaughan, publishes BF's **Political, Miscellaneous, and Philosophical Pieces**, the first edition of BF's works. BF arranges the first exchange of prisoners of war between England and America. He installs a printing press in his residence in Passy to print passports and other items needed in his work as America's first official minister abroad. BF meets the widow Anne-Catherine Helvetius and enjoys many invitations to meet her large circle of important and influential friends. Later BF proposes marriage to Madame Helvetius, but she politely turns him down.

1780: BF secures another loan from France for 4,000,000 livres. BF rejects the surrendering of American land claims in the Mississippi valley as a price for Spanish aid. Adams quarrels with the French government offending Foreign Minister Vergennes. A German translation of Vaughan's edition of Franklin's works is published at Dresden.

1781: Congress appoints a commission consisting of BF, John Jay, John Adams, Thomas Jefferson, and Henry Laurens to negotiate peace with Britain with the approval of France. General Cornwallis surrenders to Washington at Yorktown, October 19th. Due to the illness and death of his wife, Jefferson is not able to serve on the peace commission. BF informs Congress that he wishes to resign due to age and health; his offer is declined pending a final peace.

1782: BF meets secretly with English peace emissaries in Paris. He requests that Canada be ceded to the United States and informally prescribes what he deems "necessary" terms for a peaceful settlement. He does not inform Minister Vergennes of the meeting as required by his instructions from Congress. John Jay insists on British recognition of American independence before any settlement. On September 21, Britain informally agrees to recognize the United States as a nation. BF is ill with gout and misses several negotiating sessions. Jay takes the leadership role.

Portrait of Deborah Reed Franklin. Because of his many absences in London over the course of 15 years, Benjamin Franklin commissioned artist Benjamin Wilson to paint of Deborah and one of himself. The portraits were displayed together in their Philadelphia home. Courtesy of the American Philosophical Society.

Preliminary Articles of Peace" are signed with England on November 30th. Vergennes admonishes BF for the secret negotiations, but still grants an additional 6 million livres as a further loan. BF diplomatically apologizes to Vergennes for his failure to communicate on the negotiations.

1783: In Versailles on January 20th, BF attends the signing of the Preliminary Articles of Peace with England, France, and Spain. BF requests another loan of 6 million livres from France, bringing the total loan to 20 million livres. They would eventually be paid back in full, but not before severe damage had been suffered by the French economy. BF prints translations of the Peace treaty, the Articles of Confederation, and of the constitutions of the American states and distributes them to the foreign ministers of European countries. He signs a treaty of amity and commerce with Sweden, April 3rd. The Papal Nuncio in Paris consults BF about organizing the Roman Catholic Church in America. BF suggests John Carroll, his traveling companion to Canada in 1776, as a good candidate. Carroll is appointed leader of the American church and is eventually consecrated as bishop.

1784: French King Louis XVI appoints BF to serve on a commission to investigate and report on the theories of "Animal Magnetism" developed by Friedrich-Anton Mesmer. The commission, after much deliberation, issues an expose that Mesmerism is a fraudulent medical practice. BF is elected to the Royal Academy of History in Madrid, Spain. BF accuses the Society of the Cincinnati, an organization of former army officers of the American Revolution, of promoting an "aristocratic aspect to their membership." On May 12, formal ratification of peace treaty with England was celebrated. Congress appoints BF, John Adams, and Thomas Jefferson joint commissioners to negotiate treaties of amity and trade with other European nations.

1785: Congress, after a strong request by BF to be relieved of his duties, gives BF permission to go home. Jefferson is appointed to succeed him as sole minister to France. Adams is appointed minister to Britain. BF discloses his formula for making bifocal lenses for eyeglasses. Queen Marie Antoinette furnishes her Spanish mules to pull BF's wagon on his homeward journey from Passy to Le Havre, June 12-22. He crosses the English Channel to visit briefly with English friends and his disaffected son, William, who has chosen exile in Britain. On July 28, BF sails for Philadelphia, studying the Gulf Stream once again and writing his "Maritime Observations," a set of new ideas about navigation and the design of ships. BF lands in Philadelphia September 14 ending his eighth and final Atlantic crossing. He is greeted enthusiastically by throngs of people. He is immediately elected President (Governor) of the Supreme Executive Council of Pennsylvania.

1786: BF designs a device, called a long arm, for taking down books from high shelves. He builds an addition to his home which includes a dining room for banquets and meetings and a library for his 4,000 volumes, the largest private library in the nation.

1787: BF is elected a delegate from Pennsylvania to the Constitutional Convention to be held in Philadelphia. Establishes The Society For Political Enquiries, an organization dedicated to the understanding and knowledge of government. BF becomes president of The Pennsylvania Society for the Abolition of Slavery, the first abolitionist organization in the nation. In the summer BF attends the Constitutional Convention as the oldest delegate. There he argues for proportional representation by population among the states in electing members of both houses of Congress. Later he proposes a compromise by allowing each state to elect two senators. He successfully opposes a proposal requiring ownership of land as a prerequisite to the right to vote and another plan to give the President unlimited veto power. BF recommends impeachment as a remedy for improper conduct. He tries, without success, to deny elected officials the power to fix their own salaries. He believes the Convention's major achievement is the unification of states through common loyalties developed during the meetings.

1788: BF lives at home on Market Street, cared for by his daughter, Sally Bache. BF writes a will that would make her family the principal recipients of his estate. He steps down as President of the Supreme Council of Pennsylvania on October 14, terminating a long and illustrious career in public service.

1789: BF is elected a member of the Imperial Academy of Sciences of Russia. As president of the Pennsylvania Society for the Abolition of Slavery, BF sends the first remonstrance against slavery received to the U.S. Congress. The congressional committee reports that slavery is regulated by the states and that Congress has no power to interfere in internal affairs of the states. BF sends copies of his autobiography to friends in Britain and France. He writes to his friend Jean Baptiste Le Roy in France observing: "In this world, nothing can be said to be certain except death and taxes". BF makes an addition to his will, adding a codicil on June 21, 1789, making 200 year bequests of 1000 pounds to each of the cities of Boston and Philadelphia. He continues to work on his autobiography but does not complete it. The last line he writes lacks a period.

1790: BF answers questions about his religious beliefs in a letter to Ezra Stiles, the President of Yale University. BF wrote, "I believe in one God, Creator of the Universe. That he governs it by His providence. That he ought to be worshiped. That the most acceptable service we render Him is doing good to His other children. That the soul of man is immortal and will be treated with justice in another life respecting its conduct in this. These I take to be the fundamental principles of all sound religion, and I regard them as you do in whatever sect I meet with them." BF adds that "Jesus left us a system of morals and religion which was the best the world ever saw or is likely to see." His final public writing, a satire deriding slavery, is completed less than a month before his death. In his last letter and final service to his country on April 8, BF replies to Secretary of State Thomas Jefferson's query about the northern boundary "notch" as it was decided upon by the Peace Commissioners in Paris in 1783. BF supplies Jefferson with a copy of the official Mitchell map used in making the agreement, thus settling a dispute with Canada and Britain. BF dies on April 17 of pleurisy. His funeral on April 21 is attended by more than 20,000, the largest event on record in eighteenth century America. He was buried next to his wife, Deborah, and son, Francis, in Christ Church burial ground at Fifth and Arch Streets in downtown Philadelphia.

> THE BODY OF
> B. FRANKLIN.
> PRINTER;
> LIKE THE COVER OF AN OLD BOOK,
> ITS CONTENTS TORN OUT,
> AND STRIPT OF ITS LETTERING AND GILDING,
> LIES HERE, FOOD FOR WORMS.
> BUT THE WORK SHALL NOT BE WHOLLY LOST;
> FOR IT WILL, AS HE BELIEVED, APPEAR ONCE MORE,
> IN A NEW AND MORE PERFECT EDITION,
> CORRECTED AND AMENDED
> BY THE AUTHOR.
> HE WAS BORN JAN. 6, 1706. DIED 17 ·

Benjamin Franklin's Epitaph. Composed in 1728.

Benjamin Bache sketched this profile of his grandfather Benjamin Franklin, a few months before his death. Courtesy of the American Philosophical Society.

NOTE TO READERS....INTERESTED IN KNOWING MORE ABOUT BEN FRANKLIN?
SOME POSTSCRIPTS BY FRANK B. JONES:

.................The largest crowd ever assembled in America to that date, 20,000 persons, attended BF's funeral in Philadelphia on April 21, 1790.

.................Nowhere above are mentioned the names of the prominent people who came to America after contacting BF. Many persons who communicated with him made the decision to travel to America to visit or to find a new country. Perhaps BF's favorite immigrant was Mrs. Mary (Polly) Stevenson Hewson, who emigrated to America after her mother, Margaret Stevenson and her husband had passed away. She was a little girl when BF found lodging in the Stevenson household in London and they became lifelong friends and correspondents. She and her children lived for a time with BF in Passy. They lived with him also in America. And Polly was with him when he died.

.... Some traveled with a letter of recommendation from BF. Here are a few of the names of prominent persons in that category: the Marquis de Lafayette, John Paul Jones, David Hall (BF's partner), Frederick W. A. von Steuben, (Washington's general). And so did another Revolutionary War General, Casimir Pulaski, and, of course, Thomas Paine, famous author of Common Sense and The Rights of Man.

.................Also not mentioned heretofore in this chronology is the great service that BF rendered to the war effort by finding ways of freeing prisoners of war captured on both sides. Uniquely, BF called upon his English friends to free the many prisoners held in the Tower of London. His fellow commissioner, Henry Laurens, who had been captured aboard ship en route to France was exchanged in time for him to participate in the last stages of the peace effort in Paris.

.................Not covered above are BF's important research and writings on the subjects of (1) predicting world population growth and economics, (2) his ideas about the common cold, (3) his analysis of the cause of water spouts, or, (4) the possible potential of the uses of "marsh gas", just to mention a few.

............BF suggested the advantages of "daylight savings" time, and wrote about "how to swim." He also wrote about the future value of balloon flights, and suggested improving the seaworthiness of ocean-going ships by building hulls made with separate watertight compartments. And the list goes on and on!

............BF's death was also mourned in Europe. The Editor of the newspaper <u>The Edinburgh Review</u> (Scotland) wrote, "In one point of view the name of Franklin must be considered as standing higher than any of the others which illustrated the Eighteenth Century. Distinguished as a statesman he was equally great as a philosopher, thus uniting in himself a rare degree of excellence in both these pursuits, to excel in either of which is deemed the highest praise."

............This unnamed Scottish editor's statement motivated members of the Friends of Franklin, Inc. of Philadelphia, to publish this chronology. Today, only a few Americans are familiar with the personalities and accomplishments of the nation's founders. The story of Benjamin Franklin's long and productive life with his many accomplishments deserves the highest praise! Yes, Benjamin Franklin's most fascinating life certainly merits an attempt from us to know him better.

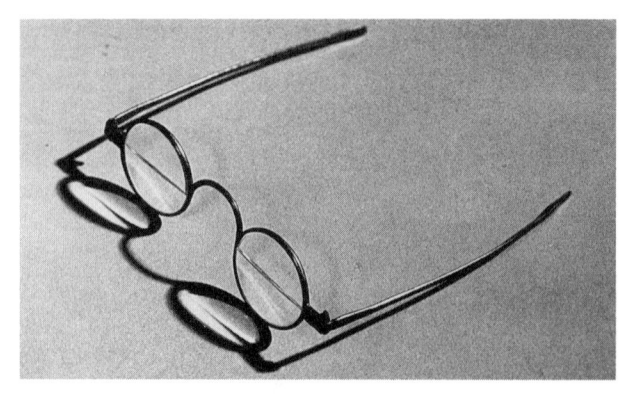

Bifocals invented and worn by Benjamin Franklin. Courtesy of The Franklin Institute.

................The editors of the Encyclopedia Britannica have called it "an impossible task" to write a short summary of BF's life. I am told that even Franklin made mistakes in his autobiography when he tried to remember dates. He was an intellectual and versatile genius who definitely made our world a better place to live.

................BF's popularity with the French women was and is legend. He honored their counsel and did not demean them. He sought their friendship the same way he sought friendships with men he respected. In his seventy-first year he was cited for his fatherly yet flirtatious companionship with the beautiful young wife of a friend and Passy neighbor, Madame Brillon. It was a happy and not really improper diversion for an old man away from the heavy stress of his duties. Interesting to some is the fact that no documented reports of any illegitimate children by BF after his marriage have been found.

A BIBLIOGRAPHY and A LIST OF RECOMMENDED BOOKS ON FRANKLIN

Aldridge, Alfred Owen. <u>Benjamin Franklin, Philosopher and Man</u>. New York: J. B. Lippincott Co., 1965. Describes quite well Franklin's human qualities.

Carr, William G. <u>The Oldest Delegate: Benjamin Franklin at the Constitutional Convention</u>. Newark, Delaware: University of Delaware Press, 1990. An excellent account of BF's beliefs and actions during the Constitutional Convention of 1787.

Cohen, I. Bernard. <u>Benjamin Franklin's Science</u>. Cambridge, Mass.: Harvard University Press, 1990. The most authoritative discussion of Franklin's contributions to science.

Franklin, Benjamin. <u>The Autobiography of Benjamin Franklin</u>. This is available in many current editions by a variety of publishers. One of the world's most important and most read books.

<u>The Papers of Benjamin Franklin</u>. New Haven: Yale University Press, 1959- pres. 31 volumes have been published to date in this authoritative edition of the most important papers and correspondence of Franklin.

<u>Benjamin Franklin: Writings</u>. New York: Library of America, 1987. This one volume edition of Franklin's writings and correspondence is the handiest single work available on Franklin; the papers were selected and edited by Franklin authority J. A. Leo Lemay.

Lemay, J. A. Leo. <u>Reappraising Benjamin Franklin: A Bicentennial Perspective</u>. Newark, Delaware: University of Delaware Press, 1993. The most authoritative digest of current knowledge about Benjamin Franklin.

Lopez, Claude-Anne and Herbert, Eugenia. <u>The Private Franklin: The Man and His Family</u>. New York: W. W. Norton & Co., 1975. An interesting account of Franklin's life seen through his dealings with members of his family.

Lopez, Claude-Anne. <u>Mon Cher Papa: Franklin and the Ladies of Paris</u>. New Haven: Yale University Press, 1966. The title tells the story.

Van Doren, Carl. <u>Benjamin Franklin</u>. New York: The Viking Press, 1938. Still considered by most to be the most comprehensive and readable one volume biography of Franklin.

The Friends of Franklin, Inc., is an organization comprising of a group of individuals who exchange ideas and information about Benjamin Franklin, his life, times, ideals, and continuing influence. Members of The Friends of Franklin receive four quarterly issues of the Franklin Gazette and invitations to participate at a discounted rate in various activities and events organized by The Friends of Franklin and the Benjamin Franklin National Memorial at The Franklin Institute. Yearly trips, following in Franklin's footsteps are also organized as well as a yearly symposium.

For more information please contact our office at The Benjamin Franklin National Memorial, 20th and
Benjamin Franklin Parkway, Philadelphia, PA 19103-1194 or call 215-448-1329.